Donated to the Hopwood Room, University of Michigan

Yasmine Gooneratne

November 1991

Ann Arbor

studies on ZONE

Alice Glarden Brand

P O E M S

BkMk Press
College of Arts & Sciences
University of Missouri-Kansas City
Scofield Hall, 2nd Floor
Kansas City, MO 64110-2499

ACKNOWLEDGMENTS

Grateful acknowledgment is extended to Yaddo where many of these poems were written and to Dan Jaffe for his editorial suggestions.

Several poems have appeared in *Black Maria, The Cape Rock, Confrontation, Croton Review, Descant, Event, First Anthology of Missouri Women Writers, The Literary Review, The Minnesota Review, Nimrod, Pig Iron, Poetry Society of America Newsletter, Sing Heavenly Muse!, Sunrust,* and *Teaching English in the Two-Year College.*

Alice Brand's first poetry collection, *as it happens*, was published in 1983 by Wampeter Press.

"Studies on Zone" received the Wildwood Prize in Poetry for 1988.

Library of Congress Cataloging-in-Publication Data
Brand, Alice Glarden.
Studies on zone / Alice Glarden Brand.
p. cm.
ISBN 0-933532-71-7 : $8.95
I. Title.
PS3552.R2916S78 1989
811'.54—dc20 89-6966
CIP

Design consultation/typography by Michael Annis/Typography

Financial assistance for this project has been provided by the Missouri Arts Council, a state agency.

BkMk Press — UMKC

Dan Jaffe, Director
Ben Furnish, Associate Editor
Kristina G. Johnson, Editorial Assistant

studies on ZONE

To my dear friends
Beverly, Delores, Elaine,
Gloria, Julie, Marcia, and Peggy

studies on ZONE

Observations

Conversations

Assertions

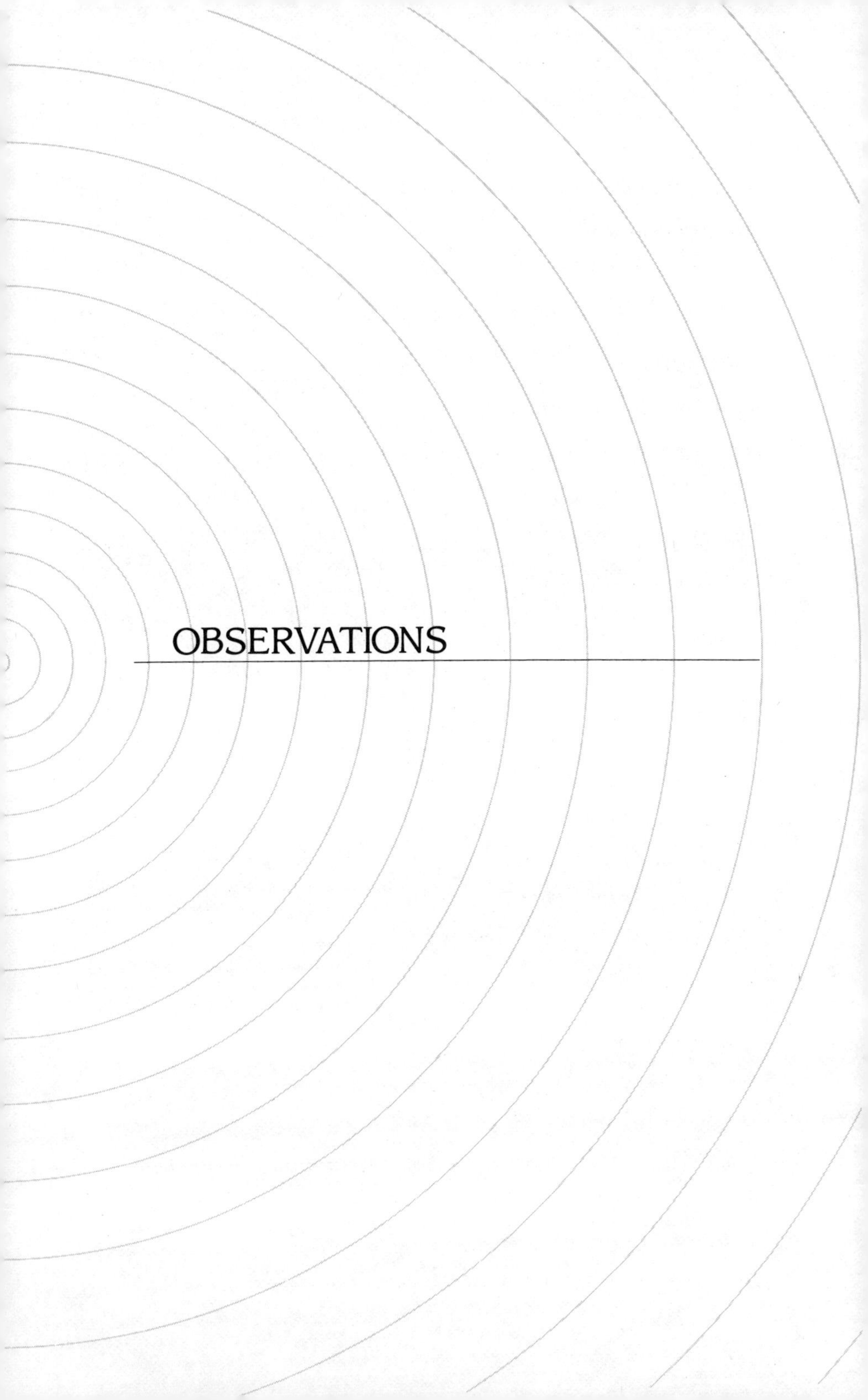

OBSERVATIONS

studies on zone

1 green minus

the Aboriginals died from measles
   or cholera or were killed
for being loud and contrary
   they speared clouds
painted their bodies
   etched them with ceremonial scars
squatted all day with each other,
   eating roots and bark worms, yams
grubs from the hollows of trees
   wattle yellow

in Adelaide they say
   the Aboriginals don't want to work
they are lazy and drunk
   they rip out their toilets
burn firewood in their flats
   they claim sacred sites that
planes cannot fly over
   they get money to go to school. instead
they sit 2000 miles away
   scheme into town for food the way
hermit crabs steal along beaches at night

2 rubble and scream

people once thought Australia
   was so red it was on fire.
it was connected to New Guinea.
   things floated down, seeds, fish,
skulls of coconuts, driftwood
   thrown up by a storm,
and the Aboriginals. bands of men and
   their families, their canoes sharp
as knives. they ate people

convicts and Jews were sent here.
   not just across the English Channel,
but through the Mediterranean,
   the Suez and Red Sea, past Bahrain,
Madras to Tasmania and Kangaroo Island where
   only the Southern Ocean separates us
from epidemics. natives fell scarce,
   entirely gone when no hope is left

coral colonies blur under water
   they gray when the tide is low
they die white and brittle if they
   are carried off

rubble still gathers on the leeward side
   Aboriginals still listen for the waters
for the Dreaming
   when the world was flat and barren
when only the gum tree flowered
   before song, before language made memory
when only touch talked

3 nerve endings, dried to broken

the Aboriginals used to poison
  the fishing holes for food.
they brought nets and bark canoes deep
  inside where they were not known
they found cisterns, natural
  tunnels to crawl down and
skulls to carry water
  when the river swelled, they paddled
down it, that brown and sluggish snake,
  trading cat claws and pigments
white meant gypsum. yellow meant fungus

only 200 are left
  in the red desert. its inhospitable winds
how quickly they thin blood to pink
  to grizzled dead rivers

out here the gum trees do not
  return after bush fires
the Aboriginals once cut deep
  slashes in their thighs
filled them with ashes,
  the wounds healing to a raised scar

4 impurities

the mountains are mostly buried
 at the red center except
for Ayre's rock and the Olgas
 ochre was once quarried here
ridges were forced into position
 to the right is the white ghost gum
to the left the gnarled river gum
 above us a sun so wild
it makes uncertain
 where shadows stop completely
where we can find the softest gorge or
 smoothest peak

today we are at an outstation
 there's a chain link fence, a gas pump
a shower made from cinder blocks
 a low corrugated building
we are told not to look,
 not to stop as we pass by
walk-abouts are dangerous like dingoes
 and feral cats and need bracing the way
horses are hobbled to break them of their gait.
 try to talk to them. they turn away
try to see their mountains, their caves
 there are no unbroken walls,
no echoes
 not once did I hear music

5 dust storms and river bone

out here the spines of the mulga
   trees warp out of control
the clouds hang like swimmers
   and come all at once as do geese.
but there is no race or water
   only a syllable of shade
and a fugitive scent of Aborigine

out here we search for rock
   shelters, a line drawing
a trace of stone tools.
   no more stories curl on
their bodies or on the trunks of trees
   no magic wards off leprosy.
there are no whirly dances
   no pebbles or shells to track
no clean up the building. yes'm, no ma'am
   no gangs, no freaks or head talkers
Negroes not yet the blacks they'd never be

they lost their plant juices and honey
   they lost their hunting land to pasture
still they stray into parks and churches.
   still they follow stones, markings,
and fallen twigs. an ocean always moves

Crossing the Dardanelles

for five hours we pitch and yaw
the young pines stand erect
other men doze over their
newspapers, their cheeks cave in
from no teeth,
moustaches drip down
their mouths thickening like calluses.

the earth ages fast here
fibers of flax scald to stubble
the fields hand up only crumbs.

women stare from inside their dark blunted coats
they fold kerchiefs back against
their foreheads, tuck them in at
the ears, and tighten them under the chin.

children do not speak
they do not squirm
they do not cry
they do not bite their nails
or suck their fingers.

the air is bent once by
astringent that
Mustafa dabs us with.
we sip farm water and suck on
a slice of pear.

the ride to Canakkale humps
over mustard fields more anemic
than the people who farm them.
like wax, flesh melts around
bundles, breads, bottles of water.
a tallow light dissolves
from the ceiling

children dim in the
tea light
the young boys sag
the men curl into smoke
of peat bogs but
the coats stay on
skin shines but
nothing sweats
on the crowded bus

our eyes burn to pebbles
and it's harder to breathe
but not once did we ask
when the ferry will come
or why this land
is so wanting

The Indenture of Trust: 1912 to 1986, St. Louis

The Wydown bus brings Ella Mae to
the corner of Glenridge.
Tamed with a white uniform,
hair caught in a net,
she holds on to the rail
and clutches a shopping bag,
empty except for a plastic
rain scarf.

She makes her way to the back door
to feed history on my block
to clean history on my block
to do laundry and hang
it up to dry.

Out here the world is stuck
on the head of a pin.
The world has struck out on my block.
A secret code chains it off
slows down traffic
leafs my block like a Thanksgiving table
wears white like a medal,
silence always serving my block.

She has taken her vows, Ella Mae
who empties the trash
and serves light Sunday supper
whose world shrivels to a sigh.
Look again, she is copper real
but bent only one way.

ink with trace of paper on acrylic

women thought nothing of weaving tissues in their hair
    to curl it while they slept, if they slept
    the rollers or metal clips
    rubber breasts in a sweater.

now young men do not want
    to kiss the girl with the padded bra
    or lipstick.

lipstick on their cheeks once
    showed the mettle of men
    rubbing it off with a hanky
    like dirt off our names.

when the real matter was to hide. it was 1943.
    Pearler became Parker.
Seidman became Seller.
    they became farmers in Toulouse instead of

tailors in Paris. it was 1952.
    you could buy a house with one accent
    but not another.
    the yellow star became brown skin.

that was the Forest Hills Gardens.
    the civic association
    Persians could. Negroes could not.

the partitioning of the human continent.
    cities, good books, friends
    barely overlapping

they attached you to us or us to you
    but only at borders.

limits of the body

the family is just beyond
reach of our hands

open, fanning
a flat sepia sky

we drift like Chagall birds
and pluck for food

the air is fragrant
with bluebells from

Goose Lake Prairie
Sallyjane sits on

the lip of the light
she is barefoot

she wears a sun dress
smudged like newsprint

her hair hangs
like drying herbs

the roof is gilded
paint peels from the sides

nobody answers me
good things fill the air

bad things strip the land
we don't know which we are.

small habits

Fisherman or just fish or just perch or lakes dripping from a paint brush, ponds that never grew, silver woods that blossom once every twenty years, a meadow of twilight.

I walk past the fence and arrange myself on a cushion of soil and switch grass. The branches of the birch spray a silver fountain.

Near Wood River a fire starts and travels for miles. I watch it clean the brush, jack pine and juniper, smoke tying up the sky. Bells begin in places with hills.

The heron knows its moment. It parades like a diva, observes like a camera. It plucks a minnow to its beak, positions it, then swallows it whole.

motorcycle

the laurel is bulkier and
more untidy than the woods.
you can't wait to grow
dill and ginger root
you buy seeds instead of
spring clothes.
in April it was 30 years.

you point out the shed
the rotted planks
the way we age, the skin
of all fruit, you suppose.
the wind reminds me of how
temporary we are.
you are tired of living
in your head.

the road is there. as always
we walk on the dirt.
you take pictures
beneath the light that's left.
you put precious crystal in
my hands and say
I trust you with it.

I knew how the house would look
the ceiling timbers
swirl gray with your hair
the cherry wood shelves are overrun
with photographs and books
your tools for looking at time.

I remember once trying out
your motorcycle
the moment between turning
the ignition and lifting
my feet. I had to trust the air
to let them rise,
the steel and rubber beneath
to keep me upright.
I had to trust cars to let me go.

I don't want the morning to come
with its cruelty of work
dog whistles we can't hear.
protect us from
what they will remember
when we are no longer
around to argue.
somebody making all
those words about us,
trailing us like
a few fluttering ribbons.

caught at the curve

at other times
the pond was still unbroken
and the fish undiscovered

we named the streams
by their lace and understood
the meadow from its blush

at other times the moment was carved
in the air like a leap

a letter arrived that we had not read
the phone rang that we had not answered
we had not gotten sidetracked by

the branches or tangled in them
we knew the way by the merest
scarves of daylight

the briefest flowering, a voice
like a distant train whistle
possibility, as free as that.

neither did she

he didn't remember my face or name
my book, its colors, the back of which he had

inscribed a generosity of wit, or
that we sat together years ago and shared dessert.

he received an award. I was awarded a seat
to his right, his wife placed at another table

her back to us. I stared into my glass,
trying to raise the Irish in the coffee

with only intention and breath.
distance is the gap between me

and the spun whiskey at the bottom of the well
but no spoon to bring the language

to my lips. distance is the span
between him and her, a felt hammer

without notes. and no moment of
coaxing will summon song to the rim.

his wife, a pianist whose rhythm I tap
but who plays to a wall. her back,
a mirror whose dark side only I saw

pressures and a loss of memory

she didn't know who she was
or why she wanted to forget
the doctors snipped a little tab of
cortex under the eyelid to fix her
this way she'd do her job
use up a day, if not for napping
for winding yarn, untying knots
only till 3:30 when things began to look better
because the day was almost dead

they took away her watch and her ring
and gave her small squares of ceramic tile
brown and white with round edges
she remembers hundreds of questions
in a small room, then sleeping
and waking in another
she never objected. the children,
she never missed them. she was taken
outside and inside, to an endless
piano and to the tiles. a tray it came to be
but too irregular for serving

she didn't know how to keep busy,
the doctors said.
so she devised a plan to kill time
it had to do with clothes
up and down the aisles
checking the racks
all the roads leading out

10 or 12 miles of web she could drive along
until she had snared every store
looking for dresses and blouses
size 6 or 8, fingering the racks,
trying them on before she'd allow herself
out of the system she invented
to save her until
she went to the hospital
to be saved all the way and
never have to grow back

nobody talks about the sickness anymore.
making a tray with soothing brown and white tabs
with no familiar edges. the tray is here
but she doesn't know how it got here
or who brought her home

traction

I cannot tell
whether it is
her feet above me
or his feet behind me
or the lymph
surging through
me like Nevada falls
I don't know where
or how but
waves are breaking
at my breasts and buttocks
dragging perfect
strangers downtown, people
making plans, making calls
people who work
from midnight to eight
people who don't.
I follow the tide
outside my door
downspouts, drains
spillways and
underground rapids
they do not hear me.
too shallow a drop,
my body left
drying and sexless

at the middle

imagine a waterfront
sails, a mast at play
    a sky resting on
    the sill of a cove

imagine Nettie in her white pants
    canvas white pants
one hip crooked higher than the other
    a sweater lingers over her shoulders
    her curls halo from the champagne air

imagine the moment between where she has been
    and where she is going, wearing white
with no sense of sin though
    white shows dirt and yellows
    ink must be scrubbed
    grass stain bleached

the light jewels her hair
loops of line flutter and bead
    the braiding of sunrise

how to keep that moment
    protect ourselves from the next
the dark lady is a moody wind
we hear fewer whispers when
    it gets dark
we do not discolor or tarnish
    no one sees how used up we are
the parts that are uneven or wrinkled,
we pull our blanket up over them

what to do with
    old people in a hospital or home
waiting for a nurse
afternoons watching for the evening
    for the edge
but nothing touches Nettie
    in her white sky and ribbons

the twist of the place

it isn't long
before I begin hating
the place, so lank and brain-damaged
like hoodlums smashing shop windows
the rains triple themselves
old newspapers look for sleep
in the basements of churches
or under bridges
there is no place to walk

it doesn't snow in February
they tell me it is not winter
but they do not tell me what
it is when only part of the clouds
buckles at a time
the hills emerald over
the sky is as treed as old river beds
the slopes fold like fabric, but I do not
learn their shapes or what life grows on them

sometimes it is not so much
the view as the light
the curious affinity that age has for light
it feels warmer with the light on
it offers more space than we need
and more water than we drink
we breathe better
we try to keep the light from going down

the fog and mountains keep us
from knowing anyone on the other side
we run our eyes along the grass of things
and at its edges
like children learning the wisdom of their hands
instead of the heaviness of this city
the fog that bends over us

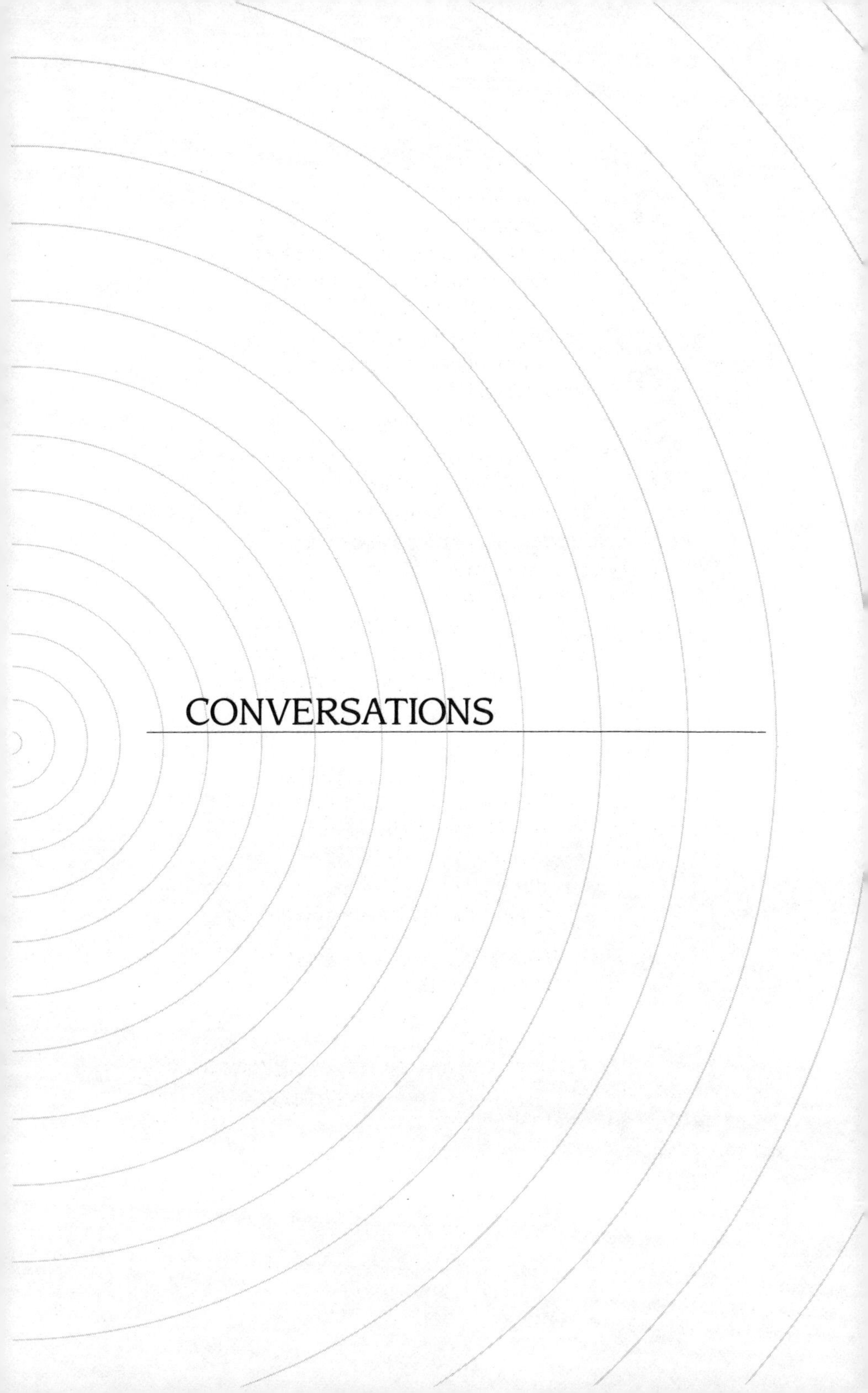

CONVERSATIONS

the village of Tong

above my door hangs a mirror to ward off
evil. red paper is nailed at the side
red is lucky. yellow is money. green is life
the family Tong sits on the floor
of a cement bungalow in a village
named for them. the museum guard has lit
the diorama for me to walk through

the perfect indifference of
a cotton rope rug. green
fringed lampshades are
not of their making
nor plastic place mats or bowls.
small squares make windows
but they are not easy to see out of

I weave nets that keep out sharks
and catch oysters for eating
pig skins dry on a line
there are ducks and chickens
there are earthly steps I cannot follow

life is full of numbers
the paddies give 2 crops a year
2 is easy. 8 is good fortune
2 8 means it is easy to get rich
2 8 2 8 means easy come easy go
like bamboo
8 8 means very rich but no
one gets very rich when there

are only 20 grains of rice
to a stalk that someone is burning
for fertilizer

3 is for life. 9 is long lasting
the average age of 800 million
farmers is 22, and whose

government wants
late marriages and only 1 child,

the special economic zones
get special engineers and
4 special things: bikes, toys,
fabric, and firecrackers.

4 means death.
the Chinese officer pretends
not to see me watching him watch
Hai Chen escape through Macau
he swims until he is caught or shot
someone says that
when he looks at the Chinese,
the way they live,
it ain't divided up right.

camera obscura

he didn't like black-and-white movies
they reminded him of ancient times when
flowers bloomed Negro
I think he meant the '20s or '30s
when newspapers were left or right
when Movietone news had not yet invented
  technicolor treaties
musicals did not yet spin on
  Busby Berkeley's axis
matinee idols were clapboard
  and Ovaltine
floozies came in Wearever aluminum
  with stark-naked stares
  and dime-store cheeks
cafe society used a ten-spot for a bookmark
the Rainbow Grill courted in black tie and tails
  and did the two-step
war was held in darks and lights
the Germans stood for death
  but not red
even jungle camouflage paled for the viewing
  public
scabs clotted like volcanic tar
  over Dresden and Warsaw
Cinerama was not yet in the picture
  where bulls charge and people duck
  from the horror and
whose afterimage persists even though
  it does not stain
repression, depression
northern skies and southern skies
poppies were charred to headstones
the dust over Verdun
the earth wasn't green till Disney
  invented it and called it a cartoon
  to avoid it better

but not yet
America mounted the creation in male and female
  a minstrel show
with no interlocutor, no sashes, no tambourines
Edward Hopper and Norman Rockwell
city, country
people left the factory in colorless cars
they left the farm, the sides of their wagons
    held together with old license plates
they went east or west, the Continental Divide
irrigation was only for water
wheat was processed out of bread
butter became lard
lard, the polish of jackboots
opinions were as indelible as death
any other tint chanced mood and mercy

the next college town

for a while the guitarists, the lead singer
shook up the space
some fat kid on percussion
how that barrel makes love
he gets punchy high and popular
from drumming everything around him
and flipping his sticks
because nobody's paying attention

we are on the sidelines
will it be Muncie
or Salinas, El Paso or Dubuque
we check out the map
which partner will pick us
which partner will we pick
and do we have a choice

if we are all singles
without the bar or bed or pad or couch
students in Stetsons, cowboys in hard hats
some in threes
everybody having sex
with themselves
with their clothes on
the way it's supposed to be
on a dance floor
when you're looking for
Chicago to notice you

draw deep on the rock group and the
beer and chips while
the band wonders why
everybody's paying more attention
to hips and thighs instead of them
when they're the ones
making all this good noise

toss a little money their way
help them decide whether it's
east or west
who follows whom
do we rent a place
finish the firewood
sell the dog
have sex without skin
like the dancers drinking down the beat
of the drummer who wants some attention

Just Within Reach

She was plain out of plumb
because see
she really didn't want
to be a teacher or nurse
or string words together like beads.

She cheated because
girls were taught to keep
their fingers on the right keys
say thank you
take small bites, chew softly
and say thank you again
to be sorry over and over.

She cheated because she wanted
to defy gravity, rise like sound
clap on the off-beat
turn on the up-beat
She wanted her picture
on the side of a bus
and came to it in a detail.

She would coin new meaning for
the spread of her thighs
new reason for the bump and grind
She'd know all the steps
and kick off her shoes
get in line, bed her body to the beat
and the beat to her brag
sing loud and turn her back on
every syllable ever uttered
if only she could make it as a hoofer.

fizz

7 days and half the sites
your triple-wide body on our
triple-decker club
sip from popular beaches
swim on a whim
a preholiday champagne package
free home delivery of hulas
deep fee fishing or
dive with scuba for skin
room on the rim of a volcano
only 24 cents a mile
rent a movie, water bed, water music
a free she or he on arrival
and an upgrade
for your dining pleasure
visit the birthplace of
the true Hawaiian lei
unlimited tips, slips, gyps
you gotta colada
book now to guarantee
bell hops, bus boys, bar hops, bar flies,
indoor outdoor weather
neon available upon request
party boats, kahlua floats
deluxe price complete with built-in luau
half-day crash, cash bar, open bar,
barbie doll, bicarb
your prescription free if we don't say thanks
every season is a pocketbook or purse
plan for paradise or your money back

pleasures of a kind

you talk to writers like you talk to fame
in tropes
you spot them through
the keyhole of your eye
not the aisle of a supermarket
you walk right by and point them out
under your breath
you refuse to grace them with a stare
and hope it hurts
to believe them is to see them in
the morning before their language is on

writers are duffle bag plain
they dress in Wallabees and corduroy
and stutter red-eye gravy and grits
fame stubs its toe and is bowlegged shy
and autographs its book with
skyscraper informality
fame hides with fanfare then glows
like the moon with indiscriminate pull.

we uncork the writer's story
and like typos we turn up
in the collection
because we have more difficulty
gliding through stage left
because we stay to crane
and snob fame back:
wit always has its way.

the first meeting of ohio and new york

you tell me you know me, you remember
the place, the year

you have seen my work
you know my sister, my city, my street

my maiden name
you recall my face and freckles

you tell me that you will call
or write or visit

we will get together in chicago, maybe detroit
do I ever get to boston or new york

you will change, in due time
you will not ask so many questions

you will surround yourself with people
who widen your way

you will not wave freely or stop to talk
you will reserve your smile

for those of certain status
you will pass by friends you haven't

seen for a long time
cross the street so as not to meet them

your door will close softly as they walk by
you will stay in small, secret groups

and nod only to special people
you will stroke their shoulders and wear their words

and come to see the rest of us out of their eyes
in due time

things you don't say during cocktails

their eyes pan like cameras
their nods mark time
their smiles are symmetrical and slick
best when they are talking
the reception is filled with them
people who shop better
whose lives reward better
whose jobs pay better
what more can we offer that they
cannot get better elsewhere
they do not know whom they are talking to when
they go on about the Pakistanis or Vietnamese
moving into town
they stake their claim and have their say
it doesn't matter whether we agree
it is enough that we agree to the arrangement
to populate the time and cultivate their soil
we do not return the risk with our name or place
we do not practice their face or their family
or ask how they came to be here also

for people who were not allowed to build

That hill is never square. tires comb
the soil into ritual Indian cloth.

The driver stakes out a Khyber Pass
at the edge of Water Street.
a cement mixer drops a
concrete circle that lengthens to
a column that ripens into a bridge steel beam
that matures to a pylon to a wall
now presiding over the grainy foothills
of Glen Canyon or Bryce.

But that's not the whole of it.
the crews flatten the Riverview Bar
like a bag of leaves. they skip curbstones
into the canal like pebbles.
they shovel with teaspoons.

They must have raised high that bawdy
orange beam, but the dunes
are flecked with only two men.
they're having a smoke, picking at the gravel,
measuring the betweens with iridescent streamers,
taking bets with a seawall
whose power I don't understand from
just those slabs.

Imagine roads going nowhere.
imagine a piece of line dragging a whole river.
imagine holding up Yosemite with a pile of sand that
merely runs through my fingers.
the foreman laughs that there's always
something a man can pack up,
lock in, tamp down, or seal off.

story of the needle

It still had brown thread in it
when she asked me to take the splinter out
she had tried twice last night
using glycerin which they say brings
wood to the surface of the skin
I did not know the power of glycerin
I thought I knew the power of my hands

I held a match to the needle till it glowed
I held my fingers close to the flame
about to go out around me and my friend,
huddling over it as a way to keep warm,
like a crystal ball plied with questions
but questions no wider than a sliver

I chipped away at the shred
I didn't mean to shatter it or tear the skin
I only wanted to return the gift of liking me
even though I drew blood and only
half the wood came out along
the stretch of the friendship,
thin as the needle itself.

as if I were the first

off Miller's Pond the field was so
   grassy my eyes hurt. when I first
   put the sky and wood together

they were sea and shrub, till the greens turned
   gold and the metal roofs wept.
   the ribs of grain bins

became circus tents without the circus,
   without the canvas, without the cheering,
   balloons or confetti

farms without people. barns without steer,
   now they stick and rust. everything is gone,
   even the metal in his words.

I saw the pattern in the chair.
   spruce and fern, transfusions of gold,
   that I bought him so he would not die,
   finally fray and ravel at the edges.

the poet does laundry

I kneel in the clawfooted tub
as if I am praying.
I attach a hose
to the spigot and spray my hair,
wash it, rinse it, wet
my face and neck before
I let my groin sink into

the water. it is quiet enough,
low enough, clean enough
and grazing the least of my
body. I have gotten used
to washing this way
top to bottom, out to in,
the water telling me what to do

especially today when the bath water
bleeds. it reminds me of that
new method of delivery. the doctors
say that giving birth under water is
soft. better for both mother and baby

if I can forget becoming
clean, then
I can settle the last half
of my body down into
the marsh licking my
thighs, congealed and bronchial.

I knew a secretary once,
older than me and with
sons in college.
she was proud she still
bled. she made sure you knew.

still I have been waiting
for it to stop. I have
been asking for years,
which peculiarity
is the first sign:
a hair growing from
a mole on my cheek or
the staining in between,
the tremblings
of a dying volcano

this morning I lay on a hotel bed,
not knowing why I bleed from
tumors that hang like pictures
on walls I'll never see,
I'm helpless to change,
why I still bleed with a vehemence
that blackens like a bruise.

silt vaults around itself,
forming rapids, cutting canyons.
I roll on my side.
I must get up
before the blood runs off the road
past any tampon or
cotton pad, through my underwear
and nightgown
I scrub the clothing,
hang them on the headboard.
I strip the bed,
soak the sheet and
mattress cover, dip them

in bleach, boiling,
rubbing, watching the Rorschachs
fade to mountain trim.

I feel as if I am caught
stealing bread, spilling coffee and
covering the mistake with newspaper.
it is bad manners to bleed
things some women don't know how
to explain to housekeepers
who share in the process
but who want me to dispose of it
in small, neat bags,
who don't want any leavings
because no one should
have to clean up someone else's
unborn, so inexorable
so final, that
in the time remaining
I miss the babies
I will never bear.

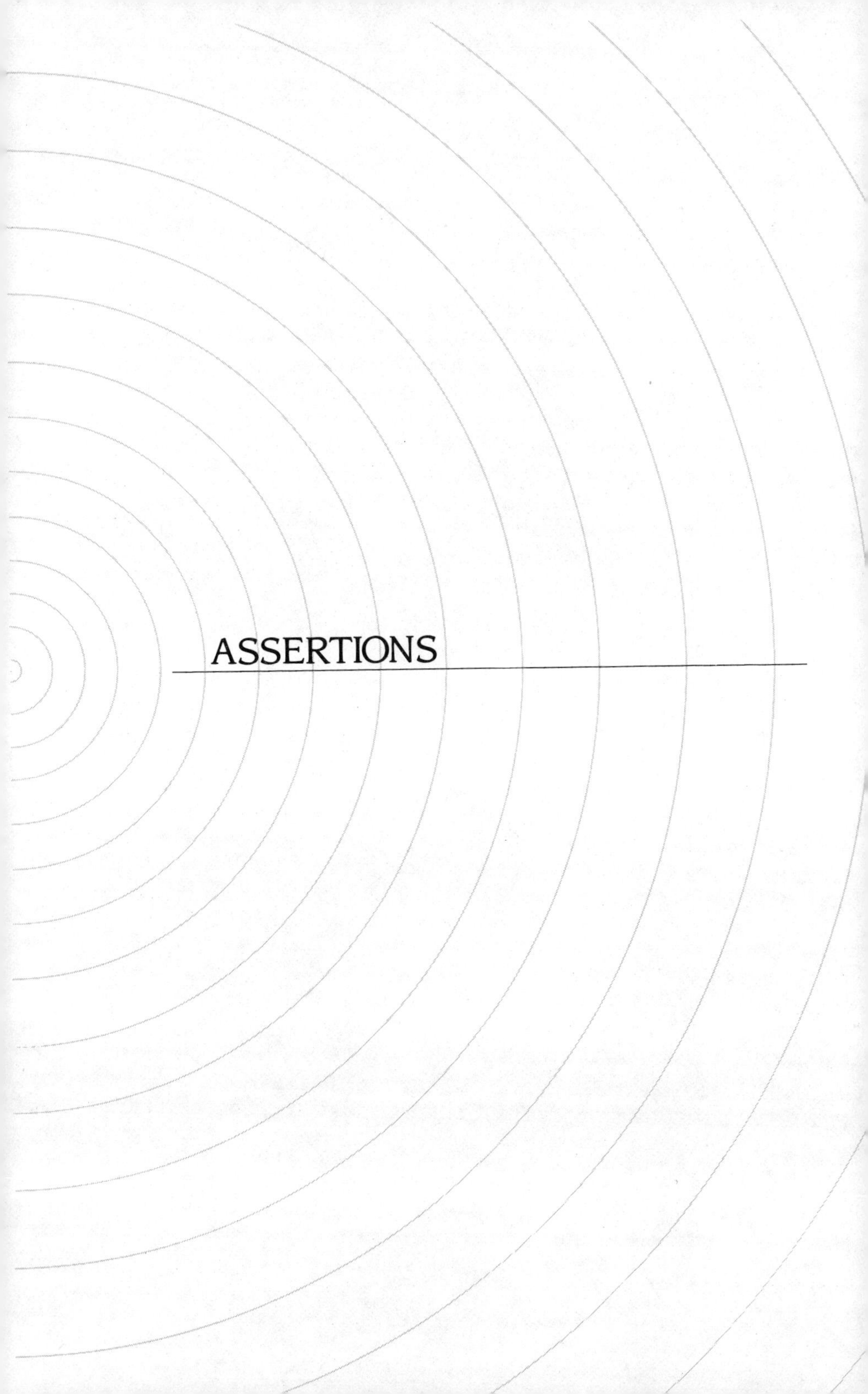

ASSERTIONS

From the Shame of 1862

In her diary, Sarah Dawson
recounts the burning of cotton
during the Civil War to keep
it from falling into the
hands of the Union Army

Baton Rouge watched the burning down the tide
wagons, carts, everything
driven or rolled.
The harvest of thousands of slaves
was loaded and dragged to the edge as far
as the mud blind monarch ruled.
They built chimneys of tinder,
lined them with pine knots and loose wadding,
so the bales would flare quickly.
Gibbs donated a whole barrel of whiskey,
maybe $100 worth.
Charlie, alone, owned 16 bales,
a matter of $1000 or more.

Flatboats were piled with as many
fields as the Negroes could load.
When they were ready, two men got on
with Charlie and towed them to the middle.

Some bales they cut open, staved in
the heads of whiskey barrels, and threw
bucketfuls over them.
They set them on fire and pushed them in.

They blazed every seed and burr and tuft,
the fibers blistering a stripe down the waters.
Like empires, whole plantations abdicated
in one sheet of living flame.
The wind couldn't launch them fast enough.
Never more bronze on the Mississippi, Sarah said,
even in daylight.

the last generation to remember

i.

each day you steal potato peels,
chicken bones, onions from the guardroom
you eat them, sell them, push
them under the fence to Dora

bodies pile like garbage and
fall out from the back of a truck
you walk around them
you walk on them
you do not know yourself until you
have been in Dachau or Auschwitz

you grab the shoes from the body in
the next bunk before it is cold
you scatter sacks of bones like
sawdust in a butcher shop
you push your parents forward
hide the sugar cube from your child

ii.

the rounding up of the children
goes on from Tuesday to Saturday
women lose themselves in the alleys
behind doors, around corners
they smuggle their children under their coats
lay on top of them
mix them with dirt and dysentery

the officers gnaw at the women
their breasts and hair, their groins
they are clubbed till their babies
are slashed from their arms
and thrown into transports, iron rivers
windowed with wire

the women don't suffer the cold or disease
they don't want for their purses
or photos or their lives so much as
for a gram or two of bread, some water.
how easy it might have been
to calm them with a sip
a mere sip of water and a space to fall

Scrolls of Fire, 1943

one mother of three does not weep
she screams a savage wail that pierces the war
from one end of Europe to the other,
shocking even the Germans.

quickly, the officer shouts, climb into
the train and take out your child,
but be quick.
her breath stops.
she feels her pulse in her nose.

she climbs into the boxcar where
her 3, her 30, her 300,
3,000, 300 thousand babies
rip at her back, gouge her legs,
the grasp always exceeding its reach.
their eyes cave into nails
their faces crumble
arms blur to twigs, to knobs,
to shreds, shrapnel,
into each other, into each other.
she feels as if she is sealed in cement
she is taken out of the train empty-handed.

somewhere in Poland, trees are
straight as stove pipes
birch and blue spruce barb the roads
we cannot tell the difference
were it not for a spoon or fork
a blue metal cup found on the slopes.
still after 40 years, in the rock bed
of the railroad, the grass does not grow.

do not rinse your mouth of poison.
taste it. swallow.
kick and scream when you are attacked,
birds bursting like sparks, solar flares.

Warning:
aerosol cans
or any container using
air pressure must be punctured
before depositing in this incinerator.
Throwing carpet sweepings containing
naphthalene, camphor, or any other flammable or
highly combustible substance into this incinerator is unlawful.
Depositing paint cans, floor scrapings, oily rags, or her nail polish and
cigarette holder into the incinerator, or her rumba, Roseland, or Xavier Cugat
maracas in the incinerator, or her upsweep, mouton hat and wigs, or her
sweater from Hong Kong sequined with palm trees, or her Lewyt, Victrola,
Brownie Hawkeye, photos and love letters into the incinerator, or her head-
aches or chills, or her X rays, CAT scans, intravenous, or her flexible
straws, walker, bedpan, or her pills, surgery and sutures, bone and
bandage into the incinerator, or her hollowed eyes, her chalky
skin and hair, or her morphine, coma, headstone, footstone,
dwarf yews set between, or the ground cover, prayer
pebbles and unveiling, ashes from traffic and
tears, dung and dust, into this incinerator
is unlawful. Failure to comply with
federal air standards subjects
the patient to fines and
other penalties.

south Melbourne man with handkerchief

slowly it becomes ours, this room,
the bed and sheets,
for days I sit here

sometimes I pace the walls
stalk the middle
I walk in and out through pores tender
to the touch
everyone knows those holes are there
the sky is bleeding south
I see the scars
and cover them with a handkerchief

all of a sudden I am thrown to the ground
shattered like a test tube,
remembering only in gasps.

all of a sudden it doesn't matter where
my glasses are or whether
the gravel bloodies my clothes.

it matters only that
they bring my children nearer
than the chrome gnarled at my mouth.

they lay my head straight.
they cut away my dress and stockings.
my breasts sink and my thighs splinter.
I have no shame.

sometimes you look at me
the part where my belly dries

the way I measure us
figure on ground
you graze the fault lines
like a blind person. my hand extends
the insignificance of ten fingers

you unfold your hand from mine
you are harder to reach than
silence in a foreign tongue
it will be day and night again
until the final shudder of sex

when you sleep, I think it
will be different when you awaken
if you loved me enough
squeezed out the bad dreams.
in my secrets it comes true

between us

if you promise to live here
and wear your wedding ring
I promise not to call your office
there'll be no trace of us
on your desk or in your wallet
not a touch out of place
I won't make a sound
I won't talk about us
to you, to me, to anyone
or ask you for help.
you can stay or go, come to bed after me,
and leave before I'm up.
you'll be proud, I'll want for nothing
I'll give up wanting
you'll see. I can keep myself as blunt
as bedrock. I'll need nothing more
than days to go by faster than nights.

words

could you look at this for a minute/I know you're thinking, what now, I just gave you a minute / just give me 2 minutes of your undivided / I know you don't have all day / it'll just take a second / see / I have these pictures of me and I don't know which picture is more me / you know what I mean / should I look polished like a sea shell / should I look rural gothic or the back wood of women waiting for food / or should I have my high school picture updated / when I looked geometric and front stoop / or should I look berkeley / harlequin hair on one side, the other side velvet / turned-up-collar-tough / hair like leaves sweeping across the street / or hair the slide of a hum / do I wear a turtle-neck sweater or a middy blouse / look I've cut down my 2 minutes so it's an easy yes or no / see / I have this sentence and all I need to know is which word fits / I'm not asking you to read a book, a chapter, or even a paragraph / only a word / one word / could you please tell me which word you like better / you don't have to do a thing / I'll read it to you / all you have to do is listen and tell me like an outsider / not like you know me or we belong together / look, I'll trade you / I'll check your words if you check mine / then I promise to leave you alone / could you come here a minute and look

in this business, mexico

no more borrowing a few bucks for
the rent, filling your fridge.
go home to your radio wailing like an alley cat.
thumb your own ride, mexico
because every day I don't know how to finish
the next twenty years.

I'm as null as a mannikin, mexico,
doing laundry in a place without a name
where the locals go barefoot
they speak as mysteriously as dice,
not minding the heat, the cystic walls.

I call. are you eating, sleeping
are you giving, are you having
hey, mexico, keep your stuff at your place.
sell it, store it. I'm worn out
being your lost and found,
your hand to mouth

I'm a motel with torn shades,
one pimply blanket,
rusty water from a spigot.
linoleum cracks under my feet
it smells as if I am cooking dust
I'm preparing my next of kin.
you are behind other doors preparing me.

How Coral Evolves

1

Beneath Mesa Verde
beneath the piñon and junipers
Pueblos lived in niches on
what was scratched from the land
or gathered in a basket.
The pollen was yellow, thick, and telling.

In another country the British
needed ranch hands
cattle or dairy
sugar caning, fruit picking.
There was always seasonal work
on the Atherton tablelands. There were
always convicts, Indians, the indentured
whatever it took to get cheap labor.

2

The winds run north and south
in Australia.
Terns carry seed.
Currents brought mud, penal colonies to
Norfolk Island and Port Arthur.
Plankton find their niche,
unlikely debris.

They grow upward till they reach
the surface. Then they spread
like a table. Pisonia trees and islands,
true coral cays. The uses of debris.

3

The world slips from time to time.
The gum, fir trees, once thick
and new on the mesa
assembled the rains, curled
the clouds like hair. Now when the sun

cuts through the fog, bone weary timbers
are broken as if from rape or theft.
If they have trunks, they have no limbs
If they have limbs, they have no hands.

4

The world has gone sideways.
New mountains are free,
slant rhymes. They deposit, fold,
fracture. They bury and lift.
On a terrace of horizontals
there is always a defiant diagonal.

5

At the point in the day that the moon
and sun match bodies like lovers,
free people can choose either.
When the sky and lake share
a bed of blue,
when the waves and fog gather
the same dance in their eyes,
free people can choose either.

They can open a grocery
or sleep out under the Southern Cross
and watch the transit of Venus,
the passage of one small celestial
body across a larger one.

blind piano player

the blind piano player is clumsily
clean shaven. he speaks

like a foreigner. plaid jacket,
checked shirt and pants that stumble along,
a child at his dresser.

in the laws of the sighted travel is forward
and back, up and down. sometimes the world

does not feel full enough. the fastest way
out is not up but sideways.
the blind piano player elongates to a dart,

a Gulf Stream within the sea.
he sweeps his arms backward, a diagonal rainbow

and it is beautiful. then he lets the
water love him like a hammock.

now he makes himself a pendant.
chords rise past him. but not for long.
sinking never fully means itself.

feet holding the floor, a body
only goes so far. if he edges
out, his music snaps.

with fingers attached to the keys,
he can't feel the things that only
blind people see.

he doesn't worry about missing his footing.
he doesn't grab onto the sides

or tread with a bamboo pole. hands are
the starting point for everything.

an archipelago forced up,

he climbs two, three rungs at a time.
his neck bulges and strains.

he throws himself into the sky like
a sail caught by the westerlies.

all at once he is the road to Palomar
that no one else ever played.

purdah,
the muslim practice
of secluding and veiling women

they sew in quick chain stitches at my feet,
the corners of their veils are held in their mouths

to remind me of where the women end
and their cotton wrappings begin.
purdah is sacred and cannot be tampered with

the paraplegic is a crawling poor box
water buffalo are blindfolded

sycamores whittle into canes for the fetid
cripples. eye disease spreads like Nile mud

the morning haze hangs like rugs of goat hair
the sun heals but the women are not in it

against their knees boys twirl thread
that trim jellabai. goat skins
hollow over drums

along the alley a baby chewing sugar cane
cries on her shoulder. still the tears
my head hears are hers

in Oujda, women cloud themselves
in haiks, each exposing only one arable eye

in Tangier henna decorates
their hands and toes. still
they make mosques of their bodies

clay pots hold water from underground pools
and never uncoil to joy or chaos

in the villages, fountains are used
for bathing, for drinking, for praying
the desert is a basket, incompetent for wheat,
where only thatch celebrates what water is left

out on the Rif, Berber women wash clothes
with their feet. veils protect them
from wind and asps, from questions
that cover me like a sandstorm

where is your laugh undulating like the palm
where are your legs that strum sitars
your rings and copper coins wound
round your hair and clapping
like the water sellers
where is the twill of your skin
your sunrise that so fades and drains away

dear carol as ever alice

I received your book, the one I never
intended to buy when you wrote and told me
that you bought mine and liked it.
I don't know why exactly when
the footsteps you hear are brush
and the breasts you grow are grain.

I look at your picture. you have children in you
you exchange consonants for vowels
scene for character.

The day your book came I pretended
this was the way you spoke to me.
but the woman in the book is
stingy as skim milk.
her fingers are clenched.
she has no body.

Let me warn you. there is a deception in stones,
a conspiracy of fields. a metal bucket,
bramble past the barn is no
different from glass flowers.
with earth alone you will soon evaporate.

Some say that having male children
makes for powerful women. it has something
to do with being casual about the penis.
you are brave. I am not so brave. do not
throw those words around you like a cloak.
homes do not make prisons, or curtains,
things female and feeling

Be careful whom you take as your teachers
they will want you to flatten your chest,

abandon your womb, plug up your birth canal,
trim your thighs, make them hefty again
with hay and corn. even fields need
fingerprints. find words that
braid like hair, that gather as hands do

holding a necklace

in my thoughts my daughters
are dancing in the Pacific
for the first time.
paper dolls, a puppet show
what better place
than at the sea, the reef flat
and the waves precious
with their coral

again, life and death get mixed up
this morning side of Cairns.
coral grows a few inches a year
the cays are so tender with
eucalyptus that I feel
I am walking with glass slippers.

some say Australia is an empty bowl,
harsh and bankrupt. so far as I can
tell, wooden containers do
important things. they chop.
they carry and cradle. objects of
daily use form an
art of intuition and love.

the scarring of the Aboriginals
the tattoos of the Maori
they take their sounds from
birds and rushing water.
we can put a frame around almost anything.

it is a risky business, this food chain.
stray dogs lie in yards or along
highways and chase us into stores
the crown-of-thorns starfish turns
inside out to cover its prey.

sharks breed in inland waters
and lurk where the sea is kind

to learn what candy strangers
lure our children with.

I am the windward side,
I am the granite peak of a mountain
that breaks off from the mainland.
I send down seed like jungle vines.
still the coral finds its way.
I am reminded that it only
takes four brush strokes to
draw the human figure.

my daughters. remarkable how
their currents sweep past me
how they negotiate the undertow
no one capsized, no casualties,
brave and cruel again for
no longer letting me take care of them.

OTHER BOOKS FROM BkMk PRESS

Paper Crown, short fiction by Tom Hawkins. "A poet's eye and heart rest wonderfully on these stories — stories which run deep and clear and are a joy to read." *—Clyde Edgerton, author of* The Floatplane Notebooks.

$8.95, 82 pages, cloth with jacket

Kisses in the Raw Night, poems by Victoria Garton. Victoria Garton blends sensual imagery with resonant verse, magically opening the mysterious boxes of human relationships.

$8.95, 64 pages, cloth with jacket

Adirondack, poems by Roger Mitchell. "Mitchell patiently stands aside, to allow these Adirondack hills, forests and people to speak for themselves.... *Adirondack* is a fine example of style, or form, growing naturally out of its own material." *—Paul Metcalf.*

$8.95, 64 pages, cloth with jacket

Plumbers, poems by Robert Stewart. "These poems are moving, experienced, and, in their own hardbitten earthy way, pretty elegant. I love the way Stewart's affection for his subject, his genuine sweetness, keeps being close-shaved by a tough, realistic sense of limits. The knowledge in these poems is hard-won, the craft impressive." *—Phillip Lopate.*

$8.50, 64 pages, cloth with jacket

Press Box & City Room, columns by Peter L. Simpson & George Gurley. Two outspoken columnists reflect on everything from art to baseball, national politics to small town gossip. With wit and candor, they examine the ordinary as well as the peculiar.

$10.95, 120 pages, cloth with jacket

Time Winds, poems by Alfred Kisubi. Poems by a Ugandan poet reflecting the struggle for African identity under dictatorship and technology. "Clearly his poetry is in the tradition of ... distinguished voices such as those of Chinua Achebe, Wole Soyinka, Dennis Brutus and Okot P'Bitek." *—Andrew Salkey.*

$9.95, 80 pages, cloth with jacket

Tanks, short fiction by John Mort. "Chilling glimpses of the Vietnam War. These are terrifying, but sensitive stories." *—Bobbie Ann Mason.*

$8.95, 88 pages, paper

Seasons of the River, poems by Dan Jaffe, color photos by Bob Barrett. Prize-winning poems about the Missouri River accented with exceptional color photographs. "[These] poems are marked by strong, breathtaking beginnings and affirmative endings ... this is a book of timeless interest." *—St. Louis Post-Dispatch.*

$14.95, 64 pages, cloth (8½ x 11")

Wild Bouquet, by Harry Martinson. The first American collection of these nature poems by the Swedish Nobel Laureate. Translated and with an introduction by William Jay Smith and Leif Sjöberg.

$10.95, 76 pages, cloth with jacket

Before the Light, poems by Ken Lauter. Three narratives probe the agonies of modern life: Lauter moves from the making of a porno "snuff" film to the murder of an adult retarded son to the making of the A-bomb.

$6.95, 52 pages, cloth

The Record-Breaking Heatwave, poems by Jeff Friedman. "This is urban poetry, working class poetry, strongly felt, carefully observed, cleanly written ..." *—Donald Justice.*

$6.95, 56 pages, cloth

To Veronica's New Lover, poems by Marc Monroe Dion. "Marc Dion has a reporter's eye for the telling detail, the poet's ear for the jammed vernacular ... full of booze, bitterness, and Irish machismo in neighborhoods 'pregnant and heavy-footed with life'." *—Peg Knoepfle.*

$7.95, 64 pages, cloth

The Woman in the Next Booth, poems by Jo McDougall. A native of the Arkansas Delta, Jo McDougall presents "the funk and smell of humanity," says Miller Williams. "Artful and serious work," comments Howard Nemerov.

$8.50, 64 pages, cloth with jacket

The Studs of McDonald County, poems by Joan Yeagley. "If there is a steel edge to these poems, there is a deep joy as well, something that comes when the place has been chosen and it is as rich and varied as the seasons." —*John Knoepfle.*

$6.95, 56 pages, cloth

The Eye of the Ghost: Vietnam Poems by Bill Bauer. "Bill Bauer takes us well into the experience of Vietnam with a sure sense of the catastrophe that war proved for those who were involved. These poems demonstrate not only craft and dedication to the poet's art, but also an abiding commitment to justice and compassion." —*Bruce Cutler.*

$7.95, 56 pages, cloth

Artificial Horizon, short fiction by Laurence Gonzales. "... a first rate young writer whose work merits attention from anyone seeking lively idiom, authentic detail and a fresh point of view ..." —*Edward Abbey.*

$8.95, 104 pages, paper

Missouri Short Fiction, edited by Conger Beasley, Jr. Twenty-three short stories by Missouri writers including Bob Shacochis, Speer Morgan, James McKinley, John Mort, Charles Hammer, David Ray and others.

$8.95, 176 pages, paper

The Hippopotamus: Selected Translations 1945-1985 by Charles Guenther. Poems translated from Eskimo, Greek, Hungarian, French, Italian, and Spanish. "A compact and elegant collection by an acknowledged master of the craft." —*Kansas City Star.*

$6.50, 76 pages, paper

Mbembe Milton Smith: Selected Poems. "A brooding soul with a brilliant, searching consciousness." —*Cottonwood Review.* "Mbembe was—IS—one of our most nourishing poets. He used language deftly, with lively, affectionate respect... His legacy will continue to warm literature." —*Gwendolyn Brooks.*

$8.95, 116 pages, paper

In the Middle: Midwestern Women Poets, edited by Sylvia Griffith Wheeler. Poems and essays by Alberta Turner, Sonia Gernes, Diane Hueter, Janet Beeler Shaw, Patricia Hampl, Joan Yeagley, Cary Waterman, Roberta Hill Whiteman, Dorothy Selz, and Lisel Mueller.

$9.50, 120 pages, paper

Dark Fire by Bruce Cutler. A book length narrative poem exploring the restlessness of a fading flower child. "A lively, imaginative and finely crafted tale of modern life." —*Judson Jerome, Writers Digest.*

$5.25, 64 pages, paper

Selected Poems of John Knoepfle. "Among the finest work of our time." —*Abraxas.* "Contains poems that ought to become permanent parts of the American poetic tradition." —*Chicago.*

$6.50, 110 pages, paper

Writing in Winter by Constance Scheerer. Includes a rewrite of the Cinderella myth and tributes to Anne Sexton and Sylvia Plath. "One of the fresher voices out of the Midwest. Her portraits of what she has seen, felt and imagined are vivid and memorable." —*David Ray.*

$5.25, 80 pages, paper

Real & False Alarms by David Allan Evans. "This book will be remembered with critical acclaim ... it deserves the widest possible readership I can encourage." —*James Cox,* editor, *Midwest Book Review.*

$5.25, 64 pages, paper